You come
SINGING

OTHER WORK BY VIRGIL SUÁREZ

FICTION:

The Cutter, a novel
Latin Jazz, a novel
Havana Thursdays, a novel
Going Under, a novel
Welcome to The Oasis, a novella & stories

POETRY:

Spared Angola:
Memories From A Cuban-American Childhood
Garabato Poems
Amazonia, translation

AS EDITOR:

Iguana Dreams: New Latino Fiction
Paper Dance: 55 Latino Poets
Little Havana Blues: A Contemporary
Cuban-American Literature Anthology

You come
SINGING

VIRGIL
SUÁREZ

TIA CHUCHA PRESS
CHICAGO

ACKNOWLEDGMENTS

Grateful acknowledgment is made to the editors and publishers of the following reviews and anthologies where some of these poems first appeared sometimes in slightly different form:

American Literary Review, The Americas Review, Apalachee Quarterly, The Arkansas Review/Kansas Quarterly, Blue Mesa Review, Bottomfish, Defined Providence, The Dickenson Review, 5 AM, Gargoyle, GulfCoast, The Kenyon Review, Latino Stuff Review, Long Shot, Many Mountains Moving, The Massachusetts Review, Mississippi Mud, Mid-American Review, New American Writing, The New Laurel Review, The Nebraska Review, New Delta Review, Northwest Review, Oakland Review, Palo Alto Review, Ploughshares, Portland Review, Slant: A Journal of Poetry, Sniper Logic, Spoon River Review.

"Anti Cain" was published in *Micro Fiction*, edited by Jerome H. Stern, published by W. W. Norton, 1996.

"The Wood Sculptor" was reprinted in *El Coro: A Chorus of Latino/Latina Poetry*, edited by Martín Espada, published by The University of Massachusetts Press, 1997.

Mil gracias goes to Luis J. Rodriguez and the good folks at Tia Chucha Press for their support, encouragement and vision. To my blood brother Wasabi and the family out in Los Angeles for teaching me the way of life in the word "enfrentate!" For the on-going inspiration and friendship, I thank the following writers and poets: Rudolfo Anaya, E.A. Mares, Elliot Fried, Andrei Codrescu, Dave Smith, Vance Bourjaily, Robert Houston, Alberto Rios, Martín Espada, Rolando Hinojosa-Smith, Demetria Martinez, Gina Valdez, Juan Felipe Herrera, Margarita Luna Robles, Leroy V. Quintana, Quincy Troupe, Victor Hernandez Cruz, Adrian Castro, Roberto G. Fernandez, Monifa Love, Sheila Ortiz Taylor, David Kirby, Barabara Hamby, Gustavo Perez Firmat, Ricardo Pau-Llosa, Ray Gonzalez, Orlando Ricardo Menes, Francisco Alarcón—in no particular order, of course.

To the sculptor and artist, Ed Love, I owe a great deal for the magnificent work he contributed to the cover and content of this book, not only as artist, but as proprietor of the one living, breathing creative space in Tallahassee where my own creative juices get flowing.

Printed in the United States of America

ISBN 1-882688-19-8

Library of Congress Catalog Card Number: 98-61146

Book design: Jane Brunette
Cover sculptures and photo: Ed Love

Published by:	*Distributed by:*
Tia Chucha Press	Northwestern University Press
A project of the Guild Complex	Chicago Distribution Center
PO Box 476969	11030 South Langley Avenue
Chicago IL 60647	Chicago IL 60628

Tia Chucha Press is supported by the National Endowment for the Arts, the Illinois Arts Council, City of Chicago Department of Cultural Affairs, The Chicago Community Foundation, and the Lila Wallace-Reader's Digest Fund.

For My Wife Delia Poey, Our Daughters

& In Loving Memory of

Roberto Poey & Virgilio R. Suárez

1933 - 1997

Contents

PART III : SOME RANT, SOME CHANT

TU QUE ME DECIAS QUE EL
YAYABO NO SALIA MAS.

—*popular Cuban song*

1
TAPESTRY

GARABATO

*In the beginning was the hook like instrument
used to cut grass & sugar cane, made from the wood
of the guava tree. Depending on the creativity
of the devotee, it was painted or adorned with beads
& cowries. Ritual instrument of Elegba, Holy Child
of Atocha, whose domain is the Crossroads.*

In Los Angeles, at the public schools, I drew
Chinese characters, or what I thought were

Chinese characters. Sometimes I copied
them down from the backs of fortune

cookies, to keep the bullies who beat on me
at bay. I told them I knew different forms

of martial arts, mainly Kung Fu & Karate. They believed
me at first, then grew skeptical over time & cornered

me outside in the hallways. I stood dumbfounded
& overwhelmed by the fact that I was about to get

my ass kicked. I'd pray to Elegba & all the Orishas
that I wouldn't get my ass kicked—as I did on many

occasions. The elementals didn't work. My *mis-*
fortune cookies always became truths: *You will*

make no friends. You will always be an outsider.
Never knowing the price, you will pay much dues.

Nothing has helped heal the mental blows, except
for this poem now & for all who kicked my ass

because I didn't speak English right or dressed
in the wrong clothes, or didn't comb my hair hip,

I say this: this poem is my *garabato*. *Con Safos*.

LOLO

We stood across on the other side of the street
in Havana the day they came to take Lolo away.
Two men brought him out of the house. Wild-eyed,
he looked across at us. Red marks etched on his chest
and stomach, blood dried on his brow. This was the last
time any of us saw him in the neighborhood. Our
parents helped spread the rumors: Lolo died later
at the hands of the authorities, hung from his cell.
Or maybe he was taken to Mazorra, the insane
asylum not too far from the *barrio*. Or tortured
at El Morro prison. Who knew the truth?
A year earlier his wife and daughter packed and left.
Lolo spent the rest of his days drunk inside the house.
Us kids did nothing but challenge him to come out.
We threw rocks at the roof of the corrugated tin shack
in his backyard. We dared each other to break in
and steal his tools—what was left of them. On stormy
afternoons we flung pebbles at his windows, broke
a pane or two, but he wouldn't come out. We knew
he was there because of the screaming we heard
especially when the blackouts started in our street.
We stood across the street and howled back,
we started to howl the day the police came to take
him away. We howled and ran like a pack of dogs
behind the jeep, the dust flying into our eyes and throats.
A year after they took him and he didn't come back,
lightning struck the house and set it on fire, a terrible
sign, our parents said. We all learned to read these signs.

RICE COMES TO *EL VOLCÁN*

the corner *bodega* run by El Chino Chan
where when the food rations arrived

the people in Arroyo Naranjo, Cuba,
lined up and waited and listened as Chan

called out "*alo, alo*" Spanish-Chinese
for *arroz*. Rice. I, six or seven, stood

in line with my mother in the shade
of the guayaba trees, watched as people

moved in and out of the sun and heat.
Women fanned their faces. Talk & gossip

buzzed like the horse flies that flew up
from the fields and brook. Chan told

stories of when the great Poet jumped
into the river and the villagers, to keep

the fish from eating the poet, tossed in
rice dumplings wrapped in bamboo leaves.

Rice. The blessing at weddings. Constant
staple with its richness of spirit. Sustenance.

Slowly the rations are filled and the line
moves and my mother and I reach the counter.

Behind it hang *papalotes*, kites made
of colorful rice paper, next to them

the countless oriental prints of carp,
dragons, tigers and egrets. Chan talks

about the grain of rice kept in the glass
case at El Capitolio in the city, a love poem

written on it in print so small one needs
more than a magnifying glass to read

what it says. Chan, rice, magic—the gift
of something different to pass the time.

Now, so many miles and years from this life,
in the new place called home, rice,

like potatoes, goes unnoticed when served.
Often, my daughters ignore it and I won't

permit it. Rice, I say, to them, needs respect,
their full attention, for blessed is that which

                    carries so many so far.

PIG KILL

the men made a game
out of the slaughter
at *Nochebuena* time—

they thought of ways,
painless & quiet, they
thought of killing pigs.

A blow to the head
sometimes did it,
but the pig still squealed.

A shot. A knife. Both
to the heart. One man
even applied a tourniquet

& broke the pig's neck.
Nothing worked efficiently.
One man took an icepick

and motioned everybody
to take note of how it's done.
He ran up right alongside

the pig & with a swift
flick of the wrist inserted
the icepick into the pig's

heart. No squeal. The pig
ran around squirting blood
all over the mud. When

it stopped & fell over,
the man said Done deal
& wiped his hands.

The men nodded in approval
believing that the best way
to kill pigs had been found.

Then another man tried
& missed & the pigs started
to squeal; the business

of slaughtering animals
is never clean or quiet.

WHAT HAPPENED NEXT

the smooth pebble broke
the breastbone of the *gorreón*
& it fell to the ground,

it's neck broken, limp.
It is my secret, I thought
& put away the slingshot.

I picked up the bird
by its claws & carried it
to the shade of the plantain

tree, there it rested still limp.
The following morning
I went to check & ants

had set upon it & in a matter
of hours all that was left
of the bird were the feathers

& those blew away with gusts
of afternoon wind. I spent days
wishing the wind would take

the bad memories & dreams:
the idea of death already inflicted.

JACINTO

lived through the War of Independence,
survived Machado, Prio, Fulgencio Batista.

In the fields he planted, harvested, fed
animals & when the time came slaughtered

them for food—a song to ask forgiveness
on his lips. He lived through the Revolution,

its triumph, its aftermath. When his hair
turned corn-tassel gray & his eyes dimmed

to cataracts, he retreated deep into a little
shack built behind my aunt's house, where

he died years later. Nobody knows when.
My aunt moved to the city & the shack

blew away in a storm. On that spot a prison
was built. On certain nights the inmates

complained they heard a familiar song
in the wind. Grew so loud everybody

heard it as thunder, the thunder
of forgetting & remembrance.

POEM FOR MY PARENTS ON THE VERGE
OF THE NEW MILLENNIUM

Both retired now: my mother from cleaning
& maintenance, before that piece-meal

seamstress work in the sweat shops
in Los Angeles, my father, a pattern cutter,

policeman before that when he lived in Cuba,
then later in Miami, his last job, a packager

of coffee, all this before his accident.
Now my parents move about the house

like ghosts: my father asking: "Oneidita,
haz un poco de cafecito." She complies

with all his requests. Is it love that has
carried them this far? Through much

hardship? My father at noon peels a new
day from the calendar, sings, "*Otro dia*

matado." My mother sits & reads
her *Holas* and *Vanidades*, smiles up

at my father who listens to Cuban
radio which broadcasts sour news

from the homeland—the homeland
that constantly grows distant & mythic.

They move through their days together.
My father collects catalogues, hoards

toothpaste and toilet paper. My mother
takes the surplus back, exchanges for food.

They share pockets of conversation.
She rubs his back with Vick's Vaporub.

They fall asleep next to each other.
Through so much time & hardship,

it's got to be nothing short of love.

POLAROIDS

The boy with the long hair smiles awkwardly
toward the light of the flash. Behind him the father,

possibly drunk, a guitar in his hands—on closer
inspection the guitar is stringless. Where is the mother?
Madrid days of long ago and these undulated images

are all that is left of such a time, ghostly snapshots,
half glossed, half faded and scratched. *Time is a son*

of bitch my father says now in front of my own
daughters. He knows they can't understand his Spanish.
I remove an image from underneath the plastic sheet

in the album my mother keeps under the coffee table.
I turn the snapshot over. The dull black surface holds

the void of whatever chemicals remain and I'm thinking
what if they seep out. If they do, what will become
of this image: a twelve year old boy with long hair,

his father intent on the useless idea of playing
a stringless and broken down guitar.

TRACE

out of habit,
I often remove
my shoes & leave

them by the side
of the bed, socks
rolled up into

the cavern of each
shoe—left there,
that simple. One

afternoon Alex,
the five year old,
runs into the kitchen

to inform her mother
that the bedroom "stinks"
of Daddy's feet.

I am cooking pasta
and I cannot contain
my laughter. She pinches

her nose. I've been singled
out for my scent, and she,
she will remember

something about my
having been there
and here.

THE NUNS IN THE FAMILY

Here's my disclaimer: I don't know the first
thing about religion and I'm not religious.
My mother doesn't know this about me,
she likes to believe I still believe, still prays
to Saint Jude for my well being. Whenever
the subject of religion comes up, I excuse
myself and go to the bathroom or pick up
a magazine. See, I don't want to come out
and blame the two nuns in our family, who
visited us in Madrid when we lived there
(thanks to them, my mother says, we were
able to get out of Cuba) but the two weeks
they spent with us, they took me to church
with them twice a day, once in the morning
and once in the late afternoon, at a time
when the children (eleven, like me) were out
playing soccer in the park, and there I was
with these two perfect strangers, dressed
like *hurracas*, walking to church. Two
weeks, and each visit they made me confess.
I confessed dry, made up stuff when I ran
out of the usual mischief I told the screen
in the confessional. The voice behind
the screen always said the same thing, pray,
pray for your sins. What sins? I thought.
Each time during mass, I felt awkward:
when people stood, I sat, when they knelt,
I stood. What travesty. Then one day,
glorious with sunshine, as we walked to church,
a truck full of bulls headed for the plaza
stopped and a bull jumped out of the back
and ran down the street, headed directly

toward us, and when the nuns started to pray,
a man pushed me out of the way into a shop.
The bull kept running toward us until a *guardia
civil* took out his gun and shot the bull
right in front of the nuns. The bull's legs
buckled under and the animal fell at their feet.
The nuns crossed themselves, grabbed my hand
and rushed me down the sidewalk toward church.
I told the story in the confessional and there was
more silence than usual coming from behind
the screen. A miracle said the voice finally.
Miracle? What miracle? I was confused
and I said so for which I was told to pray
more than ever before, in punishment.
The nuns never brought up the bull incident,
and after two weeks they left us for their convent
in Seville. So, these days when the nuns
in the family come up in conversation,
I start thinking about confessing stuff
I haven't even done, pure mischief,
like when I took off my big red T-shirt,
tapped on the door of the confessional,
and when the priest came out and put his fingers
up to his forehead to simulate the horns on a big
bad bull, I put the moves of the *matador* on him,
shouting (and you could hear the echoes
inside the basilica): *Olé, toro, olé toro*, HA!

SONG IN PRAISE OF THE COLADA

dark, syrupy elixir,
fueller of long nights:

births, weddings, funerals,
always sweet, available.

Sugar well stirred in, foam
at the top, becomes addiction,

a prayer, the daily routine
to keep the spirit going

going long after
the body quits.

CLOTHESLINES

The day my mother stood in the kitchen
                    & cooked all the turtle meat from the turtles
                              I helped my father kill & she screamed
when the sizzling chunks started to jump
                    & we rushed in to check on what was up
                              & my father told her that it was okay,
that turtle meat always did that when fried
                    & then we got back to the slaughter of the pig
                              my father had bartered a dozen rabbits for
& when we finally cornered it at the end
          of the walkway by the side of the house,
                              next to the chicken coop, it squealed & set
all the chickens aflutter & a cloud of dust
          rose in the air, a combination of dirt & dung
                              & my father got something in his eyes
& he laughed & I sneezed & sneezed
                    & when the chickens settled down the pig
                              snuck by us & ran back to the patio
knocking on its way the stick holding up
                    my mother's clothesline & all the laundry
                              drying fell on the dirt & the pig trampled
it & it made my father so angry he took
                    the wire from the clothesline, looped it over
                              the pigs neck & when the pig stood still
my father reeled it in & with a broom handle
                    he applied a tourniquet to the pig
                              & with a final squeal it dropped on its front
knees, choked by the wire which cut so deep
                    blood spurted out onto everything, mainly
                              my mother's washed clothes & the pig stood

still long enough for my father to plunge
a knife into its heart. There we stood, my
father & I, out of breath, he with bloodied
arms & myself with the pangs of excitement
in my chest. Amazed by the slaughter
of so many animals in one afternoon, I stood
there quiet, caught in the splendor of my mother's
whitest laundry. My father put the clothesline
back up & one by one I picked up all
the garments from the ground & carried them
to my mother. My father leaned against
the door frame with a satisfied look on his face,
a smile on his lips. This was in Havana in 1968
& I have never seen my father more content.
Now when I travel on the open roads of the U.S.,
I look out across the expanse of peoples' yards
& when I see clotheslines, heavy with laundry,
swaying in the breeze & the fact that someone
worked so hard at putting it up & out, I think
about how much debris time & distance
have kicked up into my own eyes.

2

PALM
CROWS

NOVA NIGHTS

Wasabi and I cruising in the middle of the night.
Downtown Los Angeles: 7th Street, Skidrow,

where we harassed the transvestites, shouted
at bums on the sidewalks: "Freeze, motherfuckers!"

No one paid attention. Tommy's Burgers for chili
tamales, Alvarado & First. The *rucas*. The *vatos*.

Everyone loco & wired out. Santa Monica, Seal
& Long Beach: sand capers on Saturday nights.

The Red Onion where the cops waited in the parking lot
for Lingerie Night to be over, drunks like us easy targets

for DUIs. We could have gone on all night, years—
Our youth spent in the chase. But what made us stop?

What makes us all stop? Hung over early one morning
in the parking lot of a Winchell's Donuts, we puked

out the door of Wasabi's dad's Nova, then we looked
out across the street where a man dressed in womens'

clothes stood by the bus bench. Lips smeared with lip
stick, the man reached inside a plastic bag, brought out

a bottle of shampoo & rubbed some into his hair.
Everybody moved away from him. We looked

on amazed, sickened with nausea, Wasabi and I,
knowing we had already died & gone to hell.

GASOLINE DREAMS

I.

you move between low riders, the Chevies & Impalas,

    down the streets of Los Angeles, the sun beats upon

        your skin, taught like a gourd, between cumbias, guarachas,

    sones & guaguancos, the music of your youth, now burnt

up in smoke, dizzy with fumes, the exhaust of daily life

    so far from the nourishment of any place to call home,

        the years gone, smoke too has taken those, where?

    Once California had showed the promise of something better,

but not really, for no place could compete with that island

    of your youth. Twenty years in the hole, first you became

        a coater of pills in some laboratory in Gardena, then you quit

    because the foreman screamed at you one morning,

& that would not do, no, & then you sold ice cream

    out of a truck, but each day started later, & soon no one

        bought any ice cream from such a dirty place, funny

how the art of resistance has been in not working,

then you played the lotto & won, won big: two hundred

grand, & so life became sweet for a while, at the banks

they called you *Sir*. You gave lots of money away, gambled

some, drank the rest. At the bars, you bought rounds,

everyone your friend. When you got friendly

with other men they misunderstood your intent, took you

to the alleys & beat the shit out of you. Punch drunk,

you staggered home each night. Once you stopped to take

a piss on the street & the cops arrested you. Sobered up

the next morning they charged you with indecent exposure,

& you laughed the hardest you've ever laughed

in this cursed land. In your youth you were the spy,

El Spia, & you thought you could be the same man

in this new country, but the men picked you up, beat you,

robbed you, brought you home all fucked up.

How many mornings did the light of day not find you

with busted up lips, swollen eyes, gone grape blue.

II.

These nights you find solace in dreams of fire & smoke,

a world gone ablaze, & you pour gasoline & watch

the flames engulf everything as you know it. You didn't cut

your toe nails for months until their edges broke through

your socks. You moved to Fontana & bought a duplex,

turned the one half into an aviary. Two pigeons lead

to three hundred. When you ran out of food, you ate

the pigeons, scrambled the eggs for breakfast. Your favorite

birds you called Solitario & Soledad, lucky birds, they gave

you the lotto numbers every night, & you played, scratched

your lotto tickets, scratched silly until the money ran out,

then you stopped making payments on everything you owed.

Six months the banks gave you, then they issued their eviction

notice. Now you sit there in the penumbra of the living room

& wait, wait for the eviction to become a physical act of removal

from the premises. They can take the man out of the place,

but not the places out of the man. At night you drink your whisky

& pass out, dreaming of fire & gasoline. *Enfréntate cabrón,* you cry out in your sleep. If you could set the world on fire,

you would. You've surrounded yourself in your own misery.

Like a scorpion, you have encircled yourself with thoughts

as powerful & destructive as gasoline. Now wait to sting

yourself with the same malice as a scorpion, when they come

for you, you will light the match & set the world on fire.

There's nothing you can do or can be done on your behalf,

all avenues exhausted. You move into your chair, sit like some

great Buddha & light a cigarette, the smoke fills your lungs

& when you exhale, the smoke lingers above you like a crown

of thorns. Tonight you feel the luck returning—you feel the luckiest

you've felt in a long time, the night will release you into a nocturnal

bang—constellations of the past, of lives you could have lived,

look around you, it is the hour of dead reckoning, the years lay

bundled in corners. Memories, soured, bitter—they are everywhere.

Light the match now, listen to its hissing & watch the comets

of immense light across the ceiling as they show you the long

way home.

LUIS NAVARRO RUBIO COMES SINGING

after Pablo Neruda

Caught between contemplation & smoke,
the pungent aroma of your Cohiba, the clink-
clank of family forever constant in the kitchen,
    you come singing.   *canta y replica*

A medley of Barbarito Diez songs: "*La mujer
de Antonio, camina asi, cuando va a el mercado,
camina asi . . .*"
    you come singing.   *clave*

Between the endless noise & clutter of this in-
between, can't-do-world, this shit-everywhere;
shit-all-the-time United States of *Los Americanos*,
    you come singing.   *guayo*

Just to kill time, you sit on the porch of the house
on Evergreen, South Gate, California, and think
about the past,
    you come singing.   *tambor*

Past the cane fields, *bohios*, the oxen carts
on the way to the mill, leaving tracks
on the red dirt of your homeland,
    you come singing.   *tumba/baja*

Bola de Nieve, a rendition of
"*Ay mama Ines, Ay mama Ines,
todos los negros tomamos café,*"
    you come singing.   *güiro*

The miniature roses help you pass the time
in this foreign land, away from the sugar cane,
sweet coffee, fields of tobacco,
    you come singing.   *tumba/alta*

Benny Moré: "*Maracaibo, este son pa'*
que tu lo bailes. En la Habana y en el campo,
todos lo quieren bailar!"
    You come singing.   *quijada*

Singing from Santiago de Cuba, Dominican
Republic, Los Angeles on Pico, then later
Plaska Avenue, singing.
    You come singing.   *pailas*

The aroma of roasted pork, fried *yuca,*
mojito criollo, all over the places
where you've been,
    you come singing.   *hequere*

You sit there & smoke & curse,
blaspheme that power that brought
you this far, so far away from *las palmas,*
    you come singing.   *trompeta*

The crystalline water and sand that glittered
with diamond dust, when you close your eyes,
the images wash over you & overwhelm you,
    you come singing.   *bongoses*

You sit there and sing:
"*Cachita esta alborota, ahora baila*
el cha-cha-cha."
    You come singing.   *flauta*

The reality of this fate, this doom
thirty-six years in the making, springs
forth in the taste of bitter, watery coffee,
    you come singing.   *conga*

The stale whiteness of the daily bread,
the snarl of this wicked tongue,
you'll never understand—too harsh,
    you come singing.   *contrabajo*

In the kitchen you sit there on your
favorite chair & listen to the white noise
emerging from the deep recesses,
    you come singing.   *cencerro*

Trio Matamoros: "*Mama yo quiero saber
de donde son los cantantes, que los encuentro
muy galantes y los quiero conocer,*"
    you come singing.   *maraca*

Far from the island of the tobacco & the *son*,
your sweet land, of tobacco & *ron*,
pretty women—no land like it,
    you come singing.   *botija*

Past the Thrifty's on Slauson & Gage,
Past the Pussycat Theater, past the tumult,
through the air, now, Luis, through red dirt,
    you go singing.   *timbales*

Past azure skies, telephone polls & all
the god damned technology of the ages,
past the pharmacies, *boticas*, and *bodegas*,
    you go singing.   *saxofóno*

To where the *tomeguín* & *azulejo*,
nest in the low bushes, emerald jungle
of your youth, you go *cantando*,
    you go singing.   *clarinete*

The burn of your song is a scar
through the heart of this bicultural/bilingual
ambiguity & nightmare,
    you go singing.   *trompeta china*

You come & go singing, through the smoke
& clarity on your way home now. You are
on your way home, you choose home now,
    you go singing.   *bongó*

Luis Navarro Rubio, at rest in peace,
flesh & bone, listen now, father, son
& ghost, as the wind rustles,
    you go singing.   *chancletas*

High atop the *palmeras*, your song echoes,
you arrive home now, like the mockingbird,
your song calls out & all the time
    you go singing.   *guitarra*

Your song calls out through the distance
of space & time for the rest of us,
for the rest of us to hurry home now,
    you come & go singing.   *canta y replica*

BURNT OUT

A man has been waiting
for his mother to die
or surpass her comma
for sixty-three days.

All of which he has lived
in the ICU waiting room
at Mercy Hospital,
surrounded by cracked

leather furniture, a rainy
television, a telephone
which makes him curse
out loud every time it rings.

He smells like a clothes
hamper, looks haggard
and worn. Some say he
has lost his mind. Maybe so,

maybe so for every time
a pigeon lands on the window
sill, he opens the window
and shouts at it:

"Fucking bird of death."
Two women in the room
who don't speak a word
of English look at him,

then at each other. One
says to the other:

"Pobrecito, esta quemado."

FOR THE NURSES OF THE ICU WARD
AT MERCY HOSPITAL, MIAMI, FLORIDA

      in and out fast
they often find it difficult
to look directly into the eyes,
patient's or family member's.
Who can blame them?

      This is their work.
Life or death, no matter,
this is how they make a living,
putting in the long hours.
What haven't they seen?

      Even when the spirit
vanishes, they go on. They greet
each other: *Empiezas? No, acabo.*
What courage? Who holds
them in a moment of doubt?

      Husbands, children, lovers?
Who tugs at them to stay
on this side of living?

LUCIA'S FATHER

is dying of internal hemorrhaging
after a quadruple bi-pass.

Here's a man, she says,
who's struggled, who's lived

hard; worked hard, three jobs
at times, welded metal under

water, slaughtered animals,
who's been married four times.

A wife per bi-pass, she jokes.
A man who when the time came

stole inner tubes from a Russian-
made truck, built a makeshift

raft and beat the odds of the Florida
Straights. Here's a man, she says,

dying, after all that, on a hospital bed,
lost on the bark of the foreign tongue,

lost within the whirl of exile. A man
beat, dying in the intensive care unit

of Mercy Hospital, Miami, Florida,
dying such an unclimactic death.

LUNG

x-rays light up
to reveal:

fists clenched
black bird wings

stretched under
a graphite sun

ghostly membranes
tough, elastic,

shrapnel
dried fruit

dangled in ribcage
Man-O-Wars

bloated on the sand
ridged like walnut shells

useless now
useless now

fibrous
satellite snapshot

again, crow's wings
no, angel wings

in useless flight

WHITE WALL

*"I've decided the only thing that really interests
me is how the sun hits a white wall."*
                    —Edward Hopper to Andrew Wyeth

Somehow the crow snuck in, its caws echo
          in the florescence of the hallways.

We are all waiting at the ICU ward
          for your suffering to come to an end.

Tonight the full moon casts long shadows
          against the hospital wall. Lung cancer

has spread fast, the x-rays show
          the luminous bunches of grapes inside

your lungs. Within an hour of ruckus—
          between beeps, ticks, bleeps—all those

white noises only discernable to the sick,
          the heart races to be nourished, first

by articles & prepositions (tell a little lie,
          call it a *Cuba Libre*, next feed

on the adverbs & adjectives, no
          need now for conjunctions. Leave

the verbs for last, that final option
          as the morphine works its magic,

pain held at bay for now. Out beyond
          the buoys, beyond where the opaline

turns to emerald green, an island
        emerges, the island of your birth.

Listen, now, a *cotorra* cries out.
        Your soul wants to make a quiet

entrance and take its place among
        the *ceibas, framboyan,* and *palmeras,*

between the diamond dust sand
        and the luscious foliage. The wind

announces your presence. Rest now;
        rest finally. A rain falls and washes

memory away to become a new seed,
        a sprout, a jungle, a man born infant.

But we return to this business
        of white walls, the crow cassocked

in its vestibule of bleakness, blinded
        by the hocus-pocus of the end

of the millennium. Inside penumbra,
        the ebb of weak light confronts

the shadows upon the once white wall.
        Your heart pulse rattles in your ears:

"*Tienes dolor, Papi,*" a nurse wants
        to know. Inside the morphine drip,

the sound of waves beckons you back,
        then the sound of something hitting

an oxygen tank, becomes the paling
        of bells. Who stand privy to the mystery

of the concave? The women angels
        come to grip your hands which remain

bound up so you won't tug the tubes
        of the respirator. Next door they ready

a man for his third and possibly final
        surgery; his gut busted and the infection

is killing him. Who returns intact from such
        journeys? Your glazed eyes look

beyond the ceiling at the black buzzards
        (crows?) circling the sky. The veins

under the thin skin of your temples knot,
        you speak by knitting your brows,

batting your eyelids, you speak loudest
        with the bleeping of your heart monitor.

No words left to describe all the qualities
        of a white wall. Thus arrives the hour

of great stillness when the distant coastal
        lights flicker down to a slow beat

on the water's surface. The heart
        shimmers, its beat finds solace in the way

the moon casts long shadows against
a white wall—not merely enough suffices in the end.

THE END OF RELIGION

When the crow in shining feather
comes to offer the last rites

& all the white noises stop—fade
into an eternity of chatter, you

will close your eyes to the world & rest.
Those of us here wonder what language

is this left us. What symbols.
We will speak in forked tongues.

We will wait for the crow to spread
its wings and vanish into the deep

blood horizon, taking with it
all understanding, all breath.

In this limbo of the exile,
this is how belief ends.

REVELATION

In 1975 my parents & I lived in Madrid.
One summer the two nuns in our family

visited for a while, long enough for me
to accompany them several times a day

to church, where I confessed twice,
once in the morning & once in the after-

noon, enough times to run out of sins,
so I made stuff up just to keep the priest

entertained. I visited church so often
I thought I need never return & it shows

now. Case in point: recently at a friend's
burial, when the priest read from Ecclesiastes:

"To everything turn, turn, turn . . . a season,"
I filled with the realization that I'd heard

those lines before, then, ah, I remembered;
The Byrds. I turned to my wife & whispered:

"I can't believe it, that the priest would quote
The Byrds." At such a moment, my wife

smiled & looked at me as if she knew,
knew I'd walk away & sooner or later

be struck by my own ignorance. Revelation:
The Bible, The Byrds, Rock & Roll as religion.

GHOSTLINESS

I am trying to explain

to my five-year old daughter

that people don't disappear

when they go away, walk

out of a room, out of our lives.

I am consciously avoiding

the subject of death. The phone

rings & there: a voice sounds

familiar, a voice I haven't heard

easily in a decade. A woman

I knew wants to know what I

can do for a stranded daughter

(a daughter I dated way back)

in Miami. I'm not so sure

I can help, would want to,

but there's my own daughter

hanging on, still listening,

hoping that I provide her

with a better explanation,

to affirm that yes, yes, people

don't disappear, don't go away

unless of course they die

& when one dies? The dead

go where laughter goes,

where spoken words go,

to that difficult place

called remembrance.

AT THE MUMMY MUSEUM IN
GUANAJUATO, MEXICO

among the tumult of tourists who hush
only to shoot pictures or listen
to whatever story their paid-for guide
invents the bodies, some naked
behind their glass casing make their stand
against time, not really, for some suffered
even here in this eternal afterlife
of chit-chatter & florescence

"Aquí esta
la que enterraron viva,
la que se afixio . . ."

croissant-like the skin flakes off
even around the penis & pubis hair lasts
& so do nails & their presence cannot help
the pained expressions of the dead
in one corner a pale faced woman
dressed in black stares at the samples
of children & she crosses herself
behind her a boy argues with his sister
that the little ones are really midgets

"La China,
La Loca,
y La Que Se Ahorcó . . ."

another guide relates the history
of the place how the gasses in the earth
preserve the dead some whose families
can't afford to save them from this fate
& so the town people, if they have relatives
here, they must pay to get in to the museum
to pay their respects on the day of the dead,

put up with the humiliation & scrutiny
of their relatives, no one is spared

"Aquí estan todas
y muchas mas . . ."

bodies everywhere lined up against the walls
vigil keepers of the narrow walkways
within the many rooms . . .

"Los Novios,
La Que Mataron en Estado...
El Feto . . ."

finally the exit, fresh air, heat & sun,
the children swarm about the tourists
selling their candies molded in the shapes
of the more famous museum inhabitants:

"La China,
La Loca,
La Ahorcada . . ."

a young woman runs out of the place
hands cupped over her mouth
vomits against the lime walls
the children run to her with flavored
water even after death, so much business.
No wonder the earth rejects so many.

THE WOOD SCULPTOR

for Elliot Fried

It could have been any medium:
clay, metal, glass, paint, paper,
he chose wood. So he sits on
a steel stool, back bent, rough hands
steady some of the time as he holds
a piece of wood. Seventy three &
he still craves the smoothness
of wood, its firm constitution,
ah its celestial scent of atoms
gathered to solidify. At night
he remains up & works best
between the hours of 12 & 5—
the most important work done
later rather than earlier; sometimes
he looks up & away from the work
to listen to the distant crow of a rooster,
every morning, the same rooster,
he's accepted the sound as a personal
greeting. Tonight like many nights
past he is intent on his wood, the only
sculpture he's been working on
since the beginning, a magnificent
replica of his garage wood shop
dusty windows, cracked walls,
greasy doorknobs, & all—
all carved out of wood.
He knows every contour.
He has sculpted, sculpted
a tool chest & the dented Coca-Cola
can on top of it, the rusty screws
created too out of the same wood
along with the yellow handled
screwdrivers, chisels, hammers,

silver nuts & bolts, the red spray
paint can. There is even a piece
of black chain & some rope
he left hanging from the ceiling.
When he finishes this,
the world will seem whole, perfect.
He carves a replica of his Craftsman
drill press, the router, the jigsaw.
The trash can by his table with dirty
sawdust inside. The GE light bulb
that hangs over his head, switch
& all. His books on carpentry.
He wants to shape the folds
& wrinkles of his apron
that hangs behind the door.
Oh the wood, wood like his worn
hands, blistered, cracked & scarred.
His eyes focus hard on the work
as he knows the way to make the wood
talk, come alive. He won't give up
until he's done with everything.
Sometimes he looks up from the wood
& gazes at nothing in particular, sighs,
day dreams. Like a blind man,
his fingers deciphering what the ridges
& notches on the wood say.
He has a thought just now,
profound & different:
If you take a mirror & prop it up
against another mirror,
there you can capture infinity,
so he takes his carving tools
& turns to work on the perfect
image of himself: of a man as he
sits on a steel stool, back bent,
hands, not steady, buzzing
like insects over so much wood.

ROQUEROS

remember the mane
        Papo's as he plays guitar
missing fret broken strings
        tattoo blazoned on arms
thin to the bones
        accepts follicle loss
without pulling/kicking out
        the jams   a Gitano cap
hides the long hair   unruly
        for the lack of shampoo
& other forms of emulgence
        Crazy Macy injected herself
last week (talk to; talk about)
        the way to the sanitorium
in Pinar Del Rio   Cuba
        boys against uniformity
boys for anarchy & chaos
        veins filled with the venoms
of everyday struggles
        soured by the rictus of living
happens men get tired   women too
        up to the neck (or hiked to the gills)
in amerikan capitalist poisons
        & the fumes of unattainable dreams
smuggled Chicklets tucked
        between cheek and gums
play chords of distress
        like messenger pigeons
that carry dead rats back to nest
        "Give us Uncle Sammy or death,
give us something to move us through."
        a few licks & the riffs of easy-to-find

blues & funk   no alternative solutions
     death on the wings waiting
within the cool lime-peel corridors
     lights out after dusk   blackouts
for the moon & lunacy of holy t-shirts
     contraband from the North
hard-core to the max
     "Socialismo o Muerte!" ubiquitous
slogans spontaneous hippies
     of days gone by *Los Beatles y Las Puertas*
Papo at the table   bandana around his neck
     next to sister   in front of propaganda food
Niurka his wife took a wrong turn
     somewhere   time to pass
take the rough tumbled with the smooth
     call it the reality of rugged chords
discordant yet resonant
     Gregorian   like molasses
who talks there? Aramis? Valentino?
     revelation hangs in a novelty tie
ah the nooses of amerikan style
     snapped Jimmy D & warped Marylynn
will do them too   more to come
     can't find it in your underwear
behind the suited man with *mucho* money
     in his hands stands another, gutted
pockets, why smile for the wear & tear
     first priority: *"La Libertad"*
no breaking through   no *kimbumbia*
     no percussion   just chords
freeze to the moment
     allegro non troppo
from the wrong side lies
     unlimited visibility
visualization   (visualize)
     rock is the thing that lasts

links the two shores of solitude
          what haven't we sworn to?
the needle, too, is a form of exile
          voluntary & solitary like all others
as deadly for those weary of oppression
          page through the mags & news
the perils of fashion only a *balsa*
          trip away to federal taxes & loads
of fees, penalties (no kidding) & kicks
          home to cities of ornate manhole cover streets
colossus among critics   a ring in the ear
          no chance to second guess
an irrevocable decision
          forced to remain in sanitarium grounds
no one literally gets out alive
          so take that imaginary railroad
take the car trip through the tunnel
          out on the bridge that connects Havana
to key west   need for sunglasses
          for the sins they hide
the restless ones have picked up
          their instruments   weapons of self-demise
destruction caught in skinny fingers
          hold on tight   we are headed
for all the wrong answers & places
          not too distant   to more puzzles
think of it as economic human combustion
          a crab in the ancient family crawls backward
through the pain   soon lights will go out
          & the night will succumb to the nocturne
of crickets & the pestilence of human vanity
          nothing subtle about the carnage
of hunger   remember
          Papo   as he plays guitar

3
SOME RANT, SOME CHANT

MAPPED OUT

for Michael Dennison

the lives we road

      cross these borderlands
of solitude & desolation

      are clearly not our own
who we are   not as important

as who we've become   the masks

seem endless & interchangeable
           shedable skins

      after each place

a new face   a clean start
possibilities dust the path

our place of birth

no longer attainable
      true   one can never return

      but the conversation

can lead us half-way back
if not conversation   then the fumes

      ah that carbon monoxide

          can help reach the ghosts

holy trinities of men   we've been

& discarded   like loose skins

    what can our silences mean
caught in the smoke of our cigars
      we smoke & ask   what happened

    the *what ifs* fuel us
      through the hazy days

& afternoons   what we were

not as important   as what we will become
    the selves of being

no longer recognizable

for we were less understood then
    less capable with words

even now through our uses of specific

details   you speak alive the man
    who set himself on fire

on the roof of a Matamoros prison

I conjure the man
    dressed in women's clothes

at the bus station in Los Angeles

    he reached into a bag & brought
forth a bottle of shampoo

which he proceeded to use

thus shocking the people
                    around him into a distance

but there is no shortage of masks

in us   what holds down the tumbleweed?
can the wind nourish us?

if we close ourselves in further

will we run out of doors?
                        who were we then?

Five years ago? ten?

our childhoods spent
                    on foreign soil

rehearsing the tongues

          of our estranged selves
          whose eyes are those in the mirror?

speak friend   the time is upon us

as we drive through the arid night
          more static than music

in the air   more like the sounds

of the wind howling us back
to remember where we came from

          who we really are   we peer

through the swirls of smoke
as it signals   what we choose

to leave unsaid unspoken

through the night
        through the deserts

                of america

the sun   almost upon us

SONG FOR THE SAGUARO

In Memory of Edward Abbey

impressions tumble-weed   first & always desert
then dust & more dust   sneaks & settles

upon everything   everywhere   cobwebs break
with the wind   sun at play   on the blue mesas

the saguaro   tall & proud   by the roadside
on the slopes   pock-marked   by shotgun blasts

birds peck out   nests   lizards seek out
the little shade   robust   proud, proud

they stand   old wounds & all   like a tall man
arms raised   up to the sky   as if to say

you can shoot all you want   but I won't surrender

ICARUS GROUNDED

one look in the cockpit reveals
the disarray of buttons, dials, switches,
computers subject to easy malfunction—

intestinal wiring gone awry
only a specialist on the ground
knows the secret of their functions

the crew: a gray-haired captain
with a few shots already in him,
a co-pilot merely a rookie in training

a navigator too young given
to bouts of daydreaming and melancholia
who feels overworked with a wife

two infants who keep him sleep
deprived, irritable and frustrated
imagine the mood of such men

in command of such grand killing
machines. Planes aren't for those of us
who've sat in seat 31E on a 727 (last seat)

and heard that rear engine die
suddenly upon a bumpy descend;
those of us prone to motion sickness/fear/

panic/prolonged lapse of reason/
madness, who need someone to guarantee
that if the plane goes down, it'll glide

to the ground like a feather,
who would like to believe that the half
that prays to be spared can save the other

incredulous half.
no, flying is too much for irrational minds
for those who hold the idea that the human

body can't survive such impact
all for the sake of making up time
getting from point a to point be in less time

airports are for those who've succumbed
to the malaise of time saved, when all we have
is time. why not arrive at destinations

less frazzled, less frayed less
scared, give us—those with the fear of flying—
ground transportation, don't believe the stats

that say you are more likely to die
in bed, in the bathtub, in your car
than in an airplane. for those of us

who fear, we like to survive
no matter what, even if it means without limbs
automobile, busses, trains—they are all safer

sure you can lose your life in them too
but at least you will, like a snail in the garden,
leave a corpse, your once human shell

thus making it easier for the investigators
not to have to look for that molar or a piece
of uncharred flesh to run DNA tests.

don't believe as I did once,
in those naive days of flight, that the safety
devices in planes will work, flotation devices

can't save you as you plummet to the earth.
oxygen? exit doors? jets don't glide, don't
have parachutes like the space shuttle,

are made literally from nothing
that can withstand a collision. demand more
security: a water suit, a casing like the one used

for the black box (which always lasts,
which is always found) never mind flight
travel on the ground, the early pioneers headed west

on wagons with nothing but aged beef
which is more than planes offer these days.
demand your money back. demand the truth:

nobody wants to admit it,
even after so many lives lost,
we don't belong up in the skies.

WEST BOUND TRAIN OR HOW ICARUS
GREW HIS WINGS BACK

I used to not fly. Don't ask about fear.
       So I rode endlessly upon the lost
romance of trains. East to West:

one umbilical chord with glitches,
       from Miami to Los Angeles,
a numbness of mind & spirit.

Over seventy-two hours on a train
       filled with the human drama
of people long gone to the rhythms.

Then the one morning before arrival
       in Pomona, 4:30 am and a voice asks,
"Daddy, daddy, I need my medicine."

"Where's my medicine? I need my
       medicine, daddy, daddy, medicine."
I wake up to the voice, a grown woman

next to me reeking of patchouli & garlic.
       Again, she speaks up. Over between
our seats a hand comes down & gives

her a tinfoil wrapped ball. The woman
       unwraps the ball slowly, a smile on her
lips, and reveals a hard-boiled egg.

She bites it, then puts all of it in he mouth,
       little yellow green clumps stick to the hair
over her upper lip. Then the smell fills

the car & people cough, become restless
in their seats. Ah, the putrid smell.
I gag for the lack of air. For the lack of air,

then a certain dying occurs—
one that can easily take place
no matter the mode of transportation.

OUTSIDE EL CENTRO DEL PUEBLO, EAST L.A.

There's Loui behind the low brick fence
some sort of Puerto Rican San Lazaro,
       dogs and all. A bitch with puppies.
       How many? No one can see. Loui

guards his dogs—they are his livelihood,
sells them at five dollars per pup. Five
       bucks go a long way with the crack.
       Loui is dying of Aids. Full blown,

bestial, flowering on his brown body.
It is only a matter of time, they say.
       The bitch lays on her side, pups suckle.
       My friend Wasabi, who works as a counselor

at El Centro del Pueblo, introduces me to Loui.
"Loui," he says, "this guy is into birds."
       "I'm into wire-haired hounds," Loui says
       and smiles. His teeth are chipped, rotted,

his lips a map of cracks. "I hear you sell
puppies," I say. "Puppies, sure do," he says,
       "You want one?" I tell him I have to look
       first. We go outside into the brightness

of a smog-free day in Los Angeles. The dogs
are gone—Loui's face turns to anguish, murder.
       Outside El Centro, next day, a group of men
       have gathered, circled Loui, his dogs (no pups),

and another man with an arm in a cast, a crutch
under the other arm, fresh bruises on his face.

Loui and the man are about to come to blows.
"You wetback," says Loui and steps over dogs.

"No, you, *you* are the wetback," says the man.
"Stupid, I'm no wetback. I'm Puerto Rican,
        you dumb, motherfucker. The only wetback
        here is you." Loui backs up a little proud,

cocksure. "I didn't take your fucking
puppies," says the man. "Where are they?"
        asks Loui. "I don't know, but I'm no
        immigrant, this is where I live."

"So do I," says Loui. "This is fucking home."
When the men realize there will be no fight
        for these two are worn and tired, too dusty
        and beaten, too far gone to get physical,

they scatter, curse, hope that next time
they'll get a chance to bet on real action.
        The man walks away on the crutch.
        Loui, his dogs panting next to him,

thinks he's had too much for one day,
and moves on to seek the shade some place.

AUTO EROTICA

Ask the man who's found in the passenger
side of his Cadillac, phone plugged

into cigarette lighter, '79 class ring tight
around his finger, the shoe laces on his right

foot missing, used instead to tie the plastic
trash bag tight around his neck, the subject

of the conversation that hinges upon the release
of the self. Some habit acquired beyond

adolescence, or perhaps before, when the scent
of panties, the sniff of the inseam on a pair

of Levis, something to undo the hold of boredom.
Something about the lack of oxygen

at the moment of release, *le grand morte*
with trash bag. The man leans forward

and thus makes it seem like the dashboard
released its air bag around his head. The man

died from such undoing. Intricate methods,
a kind of smothered-by-pillow he practiced

even as a child, the trick of a belt used as a strangle.
"A gasper," Byron called it, or rather the person

who engaged in such pleasure, the lure of affixation.
The dawn reveals the car, parked in the vastness

of an elementary school's lot, on a Saturday.
The police have come, cordoned off the area.

Later, the homicide crew goes to work.
The enema bag is found in the backseat, among

the graded student papers, liquid seeped out
and made the ink run. This is the last remnant

of the puzzle that will be put together later
in the lab, perhaps only a forensics expert will truly

know what went on here, and even for him
this will be a first. A man who's learned

to rely upon the guilt of hair, the small traces,
residues of the strangeness of the here and now.

EAGLES HAVE A REAL THING
FOR FRESHLY ROAD KILLED ARMADILLOS

Armadillos fall victim during the early morning hours,
        when the hunger pangs force them to brave

the crossing. Small, armored beings, slow
        in their intent, but bent on & hard pressed

for the promise of the plentiful—if only,
        on the other side of the road. They scatter

& move along side the shoulders & embankments,
        oblivious to the danger of asphalt & trucks

as they speed by on their way to far destinations.
        The moment arrives & the armadillo must cross.

They scurry over the warmth of the road & . . .
        Dawn becomes a witness to how so many die.

The tread of tire marks on cracked armor. Bloated,
        they lay strewn: flies swarm about the open

wounds. The rictus of death. Most cities
        employ road maintenance crews who clean up

these messes. Out on the fringes, between towns,
        between cities, between the vast distances

that link up this country, animal's decompose.
        Become maggot ridden. Sometimes, if they

are smaller creatures, like mice & rabbits, they are eaten
       by crows or buzzards. They are eaten

fast & only their blood or some other excreted
       fluid remains on the road as testimony to the carnage.

Feathers & pieces of fur tell of how so many die.
       Dogs get thrown out of the back of moving pickups.

Limbs break. Animals struggle to survive, bleed
       internally as they make it to the shoulder, then

succumb to a slow death. By noon the next day,
       in the heat of midday, the bloating leads to maggots.

Toads, lizards, snakes, all flattened—their lives
       squashed out of them by physics. By the force

of a tire. In the town where I live, it's the armadillos:
       brave, blind, adventuresome, they move beyond

their territory, come upon the roads & their fate
       is sealed. What tasty morsels they become for hawks,

osprey & eagles. The eagles perch over the carcasses
       & pick at the soft underparts. All of this plentiful

reminder that nothing in nature is wasted. No creature
       spared, spared the kind of hunger life holds over death.

SIMPLY MONGO

hands of fire
                brush against skins
with the lightness
                of feathers, slap
the rhythm
                of life, conga
the sounds
                of an island,
tropical & distant
                like the expression
of your sweat-beaded
                face
yours are conjured
                sounds of the *Siete Potencias*
Yemayá, *llévame allá*
                take me there, Mongo
ninety miles closer
                beat & slap
that magical sound
                that goes *tuc-tac, tuc-tac*
wailing to get back
                ¡Ave María Purisima!
take us back
                Mongo Santamaría
king of the hollow sounds
                like gourds as they fill
& swell with rain water
                the caress of your hands
soothes the cracked skins
                of the *baja* & *contralta*
savor the flavor
                sabrosamente

sabrosona is she who listens
    as the sparks fly from under
your *suave* hands
    to the sound of the night
as it falls over the man
    who yearns for the vapors
of gasoline and the spark
    of two colliding fireflies
to set the world on fire
    this is your sound
Mongo Santamaría
    take us back
to our place of birth
    to the woman
pasamano, take us back
    to a land that'll never be
as green and fertile
    as the breath you blow
into your moving hands
    Changó, Yemayá, Elegua
take us back
    over there to the *palmeras*
that sway like metronomes
    in the Caribbean breeze
to keep the rhythm
    going back
ancient times
    when both of your hands
& mine were one
    beat out
beat us back
    percussionist king
all the things unspoken
    & free
had he seen
    you play

Dámaso Pérez "Prez" Prado
                would have said:
ARRRRRGH! *Coño!*
                all the congas
become you
                & carry your flavor
& fervor for life
                your sound
capable of resurrecting
                the dead and gone
back to us
                take us there
Mongo
                with *salsa* & *sabor*
no one keeps the Latin
                beat better
Mongo Santamaría
                muse even to the rhythmically
impaired
                may your hands
beat against the taut skins
                of your instruments
forever

ANTI-CAIN

In Memory of Jerome H. Stern

When votes next time he will vote Republican.
What kind of foreign policy president could only
do so little as to merely reduce his sentence
from six blows to four.

                 The official tells him
to hang in there. The first blow burns. Sends
chills up his spine. That's bamboo with ridges
and knobby joints. "Fuck!"

     Blow number two blinds him with tears.
The third one he hears more than feels as it breaks
open the skin. Ah, the malice of wood.
And finally the last one falls, *swiish*, cutting deepest.

Four blows. It's over. He hung on, which proves
his innocence. Spit on all those present. It's over
for you, the officials tell him. When the official
comes by to check on him, he is still pissed off.

            No comments. The official says
his home town will have a key to the city waiting
for him. Publishers want him to write the book.
For a lot of money. Do the night talk shows.

     Fame.
There's an idea he can get used to.

JFK FOR A DAY: THE TOUR

after the newspaper story

For $25 bucks, you can sit in the back
      of an open-top limousine, a 1964

Lincoln restored to look like the 1963
      model, make your way through Dealey

Plaza, hear the crack of rifle fire
      as you drive past the Texas School Book

Depository, feel the car speed up
      as it roars past the Grassy Knoll,

"From there, from there," says the guide,
      and points to where Zapruder stood,

camera in hand, then past the underpass
      toward Parkland Memorial Hospital.

The car, the tour, recreates the moment
      with piped-in sound effects and radio

broadcasts from the day the president
      was shot—the tour guide says no one

on the three trips a day on workdays,
      eight a day during the weekend, has found

the tour offensive. Many Dallas residents
      and city leaders have resisted annual

memorials to the assassination, a way
        to erase the shame. Next year, the guide

says he will have video monitors installed
        to show the moment when that crazy

bullet hit the back of Kennedy's head,
        and Jacquie crawled over the trunk

to retrieve the flap of scalp before it blew away,
        a little extra, for the sake of verisimilitude.

THE VALET'S LAMENT

E' la solita storia del pastore . . .
Il povero ragazzo
voleva raccontarla, e s'addormì
C'è nel sonno l'oblio.
Come l'invidio!

> "Il Lamento di Federico"
> —Francesco Cilea

The President's personal valet, a sort of Sancho
       Panza, retired in Hialeah, his life played out now.

Fishing. Dominos with friends. Family visits
       on the weekends, only the few know he wept

for the third time in his life during the televised
       funerals, first the First Lady's, then his boss's.

Los Americanos, what a bunch of crazies.
       Every time he thinks he understands them, they

confuse him further. None of this sad history
       would have happened in Cuba, no sir. They took

a great man—they took him and worked him into
       weakness. A man who got us out of Viet Nam,

who did more for Cancer research than any other
       president, who paved the diplomatic road between

the U.S. and China. During those years Manolo's job entailed
       looking out for the President's well being, provide

sustenance. All those late night club sandwiches,
          the way he liked them without cheese. In those

early morning hours, they sat in silence, in darkness,
          among the tiles and white counters—they don't call

it the White House for the lack of physical purity,
          right? They sat in silence and he watched as his boss

ate. What bothered the President most was the name
          thing: the liberties with the X as they took it and turned

it into the swastika. The night they visited Lincoln
          and all the students set upon them, he could tell

nothing would ever be the same, not only in the house,
          but with the man—he succumbed to all the pressures.

They took a great man and broke him. That never
          happened in Cuba. That was the joke they shared,

when the President would smile and say: but it does,
          Manolo, it does, it happens to great men everywhere.

The long night begun with Kennedy and it ended
          with Nixon. The FBI people came and threatened

he'd lose his job if he indulged the President's fancy,
          ever again. No more such luxuries, the broken

choices of a broken man. His job! What did it matter,
          it would soon be all over for everyone in America.

The fucking past, the fucking people, fucking
          Democracy, *Democrazy*, none of it would happen

in the old country, where men knew how to take power.
          So they took a great man and made less of him. Broken,

distraught, Manolo wept for the first time when his boss
          addressed the White House Staff, then later as he saluted

from the helicopter. Manolo never wept again until
          the televised funerals with Reverend Billy Graham,

the Girls and their families now. How sad, all of it.
          Now he fishes, plays dominos with friends at the park.

They all know his story, but nobody brings it up,
          until those moments when Manolo's eyes well up

for no apparent reason, and then they ask what,
          what is the matter with him, and he says nothing.

"None of it would have ever happened in Cuba."
          The men nod in understanding. Manolo's lament,

the one he'd like to relate if he ever wrote the book:
          Views of a Great Man Broken, was that he failed

to reach over and hug the President when he most
          needed to be hugged. But he didn't do it; he held

back, and now it has become his deepest regret
          in all of American History. In America, the business

at hand is how to take great men and break them,
          break them in like all those horses in the John Wayne

Westerns, broken-in horses, but not this horse, no.

HEAVY METAL SPEAKS

for Ed Love

the centrifugal force that brings
    us to Leon Iron & Scrap Metal
on this bright but chilly November noon
    heeds the call when the power
of words fail us, our lament, when art
    surrenders to action. we must act
    charged by the instinct & yearn

for that which unravels & uncoils
    the self. in the mood to salvage,
we come in search of circles
    & signs, something to make sense
out of the heap of refuse. *cada loco*
    con su tema. we consider the clutter
    of waste, the dull silence of rust,

the blind mesh of wire-like despair.
    avoid despair at all costs, that's the goal
of our hands. avoid *that* precipice—
    for we know that precipice all too well
& often the search's all we can do
    to survive the peril of our hands too close
    to the guns. juiced up firepower,

you explain the process in *Passages*
    from the Middle: *Basquiat's Door.*
the horror of the trips
    so far taken, about to, when the power
doesn't let go. it claims more lives
    everyday, but not ours. we won't get fooled
    by charmless chain gods,

whose implements & tools of torture
                    don't change through the centuries.
shackles remain shackles. haven't they torn
                    enough tongues with the bit,
poked enough holes into the flesh, scarred,
                    cut, lacerated, mutilated & bled
                    to get filled & sickened. what more does it want?

what it demands now—what it refuses
                    to witness in the mirror of time & history—
it won't get from us.
                    you work the blowtorch, hammer
& scrape brush—weapons to break the circle
                    over the water, like the Eucharist
                    in the clean hands of a priest. you got *The Piano*

Lesson, after Bearden, after Wilson.
                    your *Blues for J x 2*, Judas & Jesus
& the possibility of both being the same
                    man. the circle's broken, brother,
but we stay afloat, circumnavigating
                    the work of the mind & spirit fused with the labor
                    of the hands.   this is greater than any power.

besides, even when the art fails us, which it won't,
                    there's still solace in the weight of the rock,
the swiftness of the stick, of the idea that without us,
                    the power loses, becomes power*less*.
the distance carries the sounds of your work,
                    as you bend, mold
                    & shape this metal, this heavy yet malleable

metal. there's nothing it can do now but give under
                    the coax of your beautiful, wise spirit.
you figure that what has stirred in us,
                    cannot be broken, what we haven't given,

cannot be taken, on this splendid day
               when we come to listen & heed
               what sorrows what joys

of what the metal chooses to speak.

MONKS OF MOOD

for Andrei Codrescu & the Beats

[Cue in]   the monks of mood
the sensationists by trade
& nature who've broken vows of silence
with velveteen tongues
who've been kicked
in the groin by romantic
semantics   who've pimped
the muses & swallowed fire &
spat theWORD
by which the world turns & staggers
& lies bisected
cubed / diced / scavenged
in fact bone bared
[bless] these boys who regurgitate
vile for the pleasures
of cacophonous sounds
cacao-cabriole-cacomistle
for ear waxed *caca* phonies
cacographers of the   WORD
hung   in the lost & found
of faraway closets & vestibules
where moths are not afraid
of balls &/or
other poisons
for they know the secrets
of the pockets   [single out]
the best of themcastrated
struggling to recreate
the bibles of *Ars Poetica*
Arte Poetica Him: Art / Her: Poetica
THE LOVERS

who died by the tickle of plumed pens
[drum in] (snared softly)
the cosmic *locos* let them begin upon
their nocturnal pilgrimages
sons of Icarus [applause]
those manipulators with their
potions & lotions & crystal pouches
from which they sniff (deep & hard)
the powder of rough tumbled
stones (now until X-mas 10% off
at the flea markets of the soul)
[purchase] hot tickets of long ago
phantoms   because nothing
matters but the fevers
that run between the sheets &
mattresses of amerika
Ixoye on Peyote *Los Humitos*
of Don Juan not the lover
but the Yaqui indian
whose knowledge filled the temples
as he danced in circles (stomping dance)
on guard recreating   the WORD
[reach out] & lick the flames
of gibberish   [applaud & listen]
to those marabarists with tricks
up the in-seams lament
for Aristide Maillol at work
on "Harmony" marmosets
chiseled in marble columns
the WORD   chewed & bit
mastoid processed   [maraca]
in the monks (of mood)
dressed in their been-through
garbs who know everything
from bas-relief naiads to Nanak
& who needlepoint

their thoughts   confined
to rummage tattooed souls
done in cuneiform not even
cumin can spice their place of song
[cockle doodle-do] the swift cocksters
dynamic duos of innuendo
& free verse   who during the last
solstice doused their flesh
with their spouses amniotic fluids
who've parachuted over desert(ed)
minds & landed on saguaros
& chollas   who've been pricked
stung / pierced by minds
bonsai-ed / boomeranged
between two ideas yin-yanging
who've dared ask why the male
bobolink is more magnificent
than the female the *sus scrofa* sisters
& their carnivorous appetites
don't care too much
for this song & dance
they much rather apply Occam's Razor
to all problems & concerns with the WORD
Ok [clue] the monks of mood &
their funked up blues   confiscate
them from their hideaways
(metropolis) & render them impotent
[catch] them in penumbra these lovers
of umbrellas left opened indoors
[bless] them for their misplaced intellect
[give] them the flow of elixir
(Corona, the Mexican beer of Choice—
La Mas Fina!) or [let] them
suck on *gusanos* (Maguey worms)
Mescal for they belong in other places
[bring] them zithers or zinnias

either will do to turn the magic
of the dust & powder & work
with the WORD
their spells on you

ODE TO A TORCH SONG GIRL

for Vance Bourjaily

here we go

born out of sand & soft mud
& prickly pears & monsoons
one cool windy afternoon

O Tucson city of spirits long
turned to rubble & dust & grass
& red earth as we travel
in a U-Haul rental truck
with enough space for dead
rooms & spineless chairs
a couple on the move
"*All needed, or is there more?*"
off down ruin river of tar &
encrusted carcasses & rain
the truck becomes a red
speck where the blue of the sky
meets brown ground caught
in splendor among the tall weeds
& pastures & rockbeds

O Tucson city
leaden with dead indian
& blood evaporated in the heat
of the moon & its silk
a latent straw wine young
woman who wore
much silver at bay fights
unhappy last week
prickles navel windy with pleasure

"*No fury in hell like goat's milk*"
bourbon breath & crooked sheets
between her legs an empty
champagne goblet oozing glitter

O girl whose skies
stick out at angles
affirms the beast insincere in me
truck tugging Plymouth green
& crankshaftless
motor oil veins on the divided
asphalt wheels hum & buzz
a scorpion malice
so many lives destroyed
& more on the brink
this road connects west & east
with a single thread of loneliness
& disillusion interstate 10
"*Shall we stop for coffee*
or iced tea? sleep   sleep
in dead hour `NO TELL' motels
& forget from where
the wind blew us like tumbleweeds?"
quick conversation fades
out of windows
sometimes creeps like a priest
into the confessional

O girl you cannot breathe
poppies through my veins
& expect balloons to pop
in the circus of my mind
for there can be no other
moments like these when your tongue
vacuum cleans those vast areas of my dust

& slopes of grey skin to distant shadows
arrival time in Baton Rouge 2 days
of sleeplessness
hits the somnambulist across the groin
Texas nothing but a huge grease spot
on the stained map
"*See? Baton Rouge across the river?*"
eyes as muddy as this water
humidity pebbles on skin
quickly de/attach to new circumstances
WELCOME TO LOUISIANA
land of the low kudzu & Spanish moss
& mosquitos the size
of syringes hide in the emerald
a flat wheel hums
swamp-swampitty-swamp
bridges may ice in cold weather
WELCOME!
in this city life lingers
sluggish beat to slow beat
across nowhere
past SPARE LIMBS & OTHER AIDS
out of the desert & thirst for water
that'll never be as clean
& clear & yearn for a way
to be   somewhere
else   (anywhere)
within city limits now
in the brick temples of God
Sunday voices sound fortissimo
"*Lord BE lord ALL lorn MINE!*"
each stained glass window
shows the tomb from which Christ
rose to meet the sparrows
that drink the dew from his flesh
roll down the window & hear

listen to the sleet rain shout
"*Succumb to the succubus*"
& skid around corners

O girl   a priest
with enormous wings
whose pecker a leper once plucked
warned that unmarried
cohabitators be damned
should marry us
so that our vows may hover
over our heads
in the pursuit of nothing

there we go

NOTES & TRANSLATIONS

p 13   *garabato* is also literally a scribble, there's some of that meaning intended in the poem.

p 14   *Con Safos*: Of Chicano origin, a safety precaution. In the words of José Antonio Burciaga, it is a barrio copyright . . . no one else could use or dishonor with graffiti, "anything you say against me will bounce back to you." For lengthy discussion of the term read *Drink Cultura* by José Antonio Burciaga, published by Odell Editions/Santa Barbara, 1993.

p 15   *barrio*: neighborhood.

p 16   *bodega*: market.

p 18   *Nochebuena*: Christmas eve. For Cubans it is the most festive of nights, and usually on the menu is a pig barbecued in a backyard pit.

p 20   *gorreón*: a sparrow.

p 21   Machado, Prio, Fulgencio Batista: presidents turned dictators in Cuba during the 30's, 40's, and 50's.

p 22   *Haz un poco the cafecito*: Brew a little coffee.

   Otro dia matado: Another day killed.

   Hola & Vanidades: gossip/fashion magazines in Spanish.

p 26-27   *hurracas*: magpies

   guardia civil: Spanish policeman

   matador: bullfighter

   Olé toro: what a bullfighter says to make the bull charge.

p 28   A *colada* is machine brewed Cuban coffee, approximately two ounces or five thimble-sized servings, enough to keep the uninitiated energized for hours.

p 33 *rucas, vatos*: Mexican slang for girlfriend or chick and guys or home boys.

p 34-37 *cumbias, guarachas, sones* and *guaguancos*: all music originating in Latin America and Cuba.

El spia: the spy.

Enfrentate cabrón: show your face, you bastard.

p 38-41 *clave, guayo, tambor, tumba/baja, güiro, tumba/alta, quijada, pailas, chequere, bongoses, conga, cencerro, maraca, botija, timbales, bongo, chancletas*: all percussion instruments.

Canta y replica: sing and reply.

La mujer de Antonio, camina asi, cuando va a el mercado, camina asi: Antonio's wife, she walks like this, when she goes to the market, she walk's like this. Song written by Trío Matamoros, performed by Barbarito Diez.

Los Americanos: The Americans.

Bohios: Thatched huts.

Ay mama Ines, Ay mama Ines, todos los negros tomamos café: Oh mama Ines, Oh mama Ines, all of us blacks like to drink coffee. Origin in Cuban folk songs.

Maracaibo, este son pa que tu lo bailes. En la Habana y en el campo, todos lo quieren bailar: Maracaibo, this son so you can dance to it. In Havana and in the fields, everyone wants to dance to it. "Maracaibo Oriental" a song written by José A. Castañeda and performed by Benny Moré.

Son: a type of Cuban song.

Yuca: cassava, a tuber.

Mojito criollo: a tropical marinade sauce.

Las palmas: the palm trees.

Cachita esta alborota, ahora baila el cha-cha-cha: Cachita (Barbara) is excited, now she dances the cha-cha-cha. *Mama yo quiero saber de donde son los cantantes, que los encuentro muy galantes y los quiero conocer*: Mother I want to know where singers are from, I find them quite gallant and I want to know them. "Son de la Loma" a song written and performed by Trío Matamoros.

Ron: rum.

Boticas and *bodegas*: a type of drugstore and store or market.

Tomeguín and *azulejo*: a Cuban green singing finch and a Cuban blue bird.

Palmeras: palm trees.

p 42   *Pobrecito, esta quemado*: Poor thing, he's burnt out.

p 43   *Empiezas? No, acabo*: Are you beginning? No, ending.

p 46-48   *Cotorra*: a Cuban parrot.

Ceibas, framboyan, and *palmeras*: types of trees native and imported that grow abundant in Cuba.

Tienes dolor, Papi: Do you have pain, Papi?

p 53-54   *Aqui esta la que enterraron viva, la que se afixió*: Here is the one buried alive, the one who died of asphyxiation.

La China, La Loca, y La Que Se Ahorco: The Chinese Woman, The Crazy Woman, The One Who Hung Herself.

Aqui estan todas y muchas mas: Here they are and many more.

Los Novios, La Que Mataron en Estado . . . El Feto: The Lovers, The One They Killed Pregnant . . . The Fetus.

p 57-59 *Socialismo o Muerte*: Socialism or Death! A Cuban rally-to-arms slogan.

Los Beatles y Las Puertas: The Beatles and The Doors.

La Libertad: Lady Liberty; freedom.

Kimbumbia: a game played with three sticks.

Balsa: a raft. (More Cubans have lost their lives in the Florida Straights crossing on these make-shift vessels than those who have completed the journey.)

p 73 San Lazaro, St. Lazarus: the figure appearing in the parable of the rich man and the beggar, not an official Catholic saint. (Babalú Ayé in the Afro-Cuban pantheon.)

p 79-81 *Siete Potencias*: The Seven Afro-Cuban Deities.

Llévame allá: Take me there.

Ave María Purisima: Blessed Virgin Mary.

Baja and contralta: percussion instruments (congas, tumbadoras).

Sabrosamente, sabrosona: deliciously, delicious like a woman.

Suave: soft.

Pasamano: a person who heals with the hands.

Changó, Yemayá, Elegua (Shango, Yemaya, Elegba): African-Cuban Deities.

Dámaso Pérez "Prez" Prado: the other mambo king. Benny Moré was the King.

Coño: Cuban expression of awe, also used for emphasis.

Salsa and *sabor*: not only the dance but the sauce and flavor.

p 85   Translation of the epigram from "Il Lamento di Federico
        from Francesco Cilea's L'ARLESIANA: "It's the usual story
        of the shepherd . . . / The poor boy wanted to say it, / but
        fell asleep. / In sleep there is oblivion. / How I envy him!"

p 88   *Cada loco con su tema*: Each crazy person with his or her
        own theme.

p 93   *La Mas Fina*: The finest.